Linking art to the world

artyfacts

Plants

Abbey
Children's
Books

CONCEPT

Publisher: Felicia Law

Design: Tracy Carrington

Editorial Planning: Karen Foster

Research and Development: Gerry Bailey, Alec Edgington

PROJECT DEVELOPMENT

Project Director: Karen Foster

Editors: Claire Sipi, Hazel Songhurst, Samantha Sweeney

Design Director: Tracy Carrington

Design Manager: Flora Awolaja

Design and DTP: Claire Penny, Paul Montague,
James Thompson, Mark Dempsey

Photo and Art Editor: Andrea Sadler

Illustrator: Jan Smith

Model Artist: Sophie Dean

Further models: Sue Partington, Abigail Dean, Harry Foster

Digital Workflow: Edward MacDermott

Production: Victoria Grimsell, Christina Brown

Scanning: Acumen Colour Ltd

Published by Abbey Children's Books
(a division of Abbey Home Media Group)

Abbey Home Media Group
435-437 Edgware Road
London W2 1TH
United Kingdom

Printed and bound by Dai Nippon, Hong Kong

Linking art to the world around us

artyfacts
Plants

Contents

WRITTEN BY Rosie McCormick

Leaves

Leaves are like very small food factories. Their job is to change sunlight, water and carbon dioxide into food to help the plant grow. Different plants have different leaves which vary in shape, size, texture and pattern.

CHLOROPLASTS

Leaves are usually green. This is because their cells contain tiny green parts called chloroplasts. Each chloroplast contains a green substance called chlorophyll.

PHOTOSYNTHESIS

The chloroplasts use sunlight, carbon dioxide and water to make food. Sunlight enters the leaf through its clear, outer cells. Water comes to the leaf from the soil, through the roots and stem of the plant. Air, which contains the gas carbon dioxide, enters through tiny openings called stomata in the leaf's surface. Inside the chloroplasts, the chlorophyll uses the sunlight's energy to combine the water and carbon dioxide and change them into sugars. This process is called 'photosynthesis'. The sugars are then turned into starch. Tiny pieces of starch are stored in the cells of the leaf and used as food.

FALLING LEAVES

In autumn, leaves growing on deciduous trees start to die. They change to yellow or brown before falling to the ground. Trees that keep their green leaves all year round are called evergreens.

Plants

WHAT YOU NEED

scissors

double-sided sticky tape

card and paper

newspaper

masking tape

pencil

poster paint

plastic tray

glue

coloured wax crayons

mounting card

leaves

Leaf print patterns

Make a colourful leafy collage with your prints

1 Collect a variety of leaves from the garden or park.

2 On a piece of card, draw around each leaf.

3 Cut out your leaf shapes. Cover the table with newspaper.

4 Put some paint in a tray. Dip your leaf shapes in the paint.

5 Put the leaf shapes on the mounting card. Place another piece of paper over the top of them and gently rub over the shapes.

Remove the paper and leaf shapes to reveal the prints.

6

Leaf rubbings

Using double-sided tape, stick the leaves smooth side down onto a hard surface. Lay a piece of thin paper on top, taped down with masking tape. Gently rub across the paper with wax crayons. When the leaf patterns show clearly, cut them out and stick them onto black mounting card.

Caps and stalks

Fungi just love damp, dark surroundings and places where most green plants can't grow. They feed on living things or dead and rotting plants through long, thin feeding threads hidden in the ground. The parts of fungi you can see – the caps and stalks of toadstools and mushrooms for example – come in amazing shapes, sizes and colours. They can be smaller than the tip of a needle or bigger than a watermelon.

ANYTHING BUT GREEN

Fungi can be many different colours. They can be bright red like the fly algaric toadstool or silvery-grey like the delicate puffball, but they are rarely green. This is because they do not contain chlorophyll, the green pigment plants use to make food from sunlight.

PUFFBALLS

Fungi make spores, which grow into new fungi. A spore is like a seed, but it is smaller and simpler. Mushroom spores grow in the fragile walls called gills beneath the umbrella-shaped top or cap. Puffball spores develop inside a bag-like chamber. If a raindrop gently plops on to a puffball, a little cloud of spores puffs out of a tiny hole. Most fungi release their spores into the air. Because they are so light, the spores travel a long way. When a spore lands in a suitable place, it grows into a new fungus.

FAIRY RINGS

A fairy ring is a small group of mushrooms growing in a circle in a field or grassy area. Although it is made up of separate mushrooms, they are all part of the same fungus. People once believed fairies created fairy rings, because they look so magical.

MUSHROOM OR TOADSTOOL?

Mushrooms are edible but toadstools are poisonous. So never touch or eat wild fungi.

Spore prints

You can print up a masterpiece with mushrooms!

WHAT YOU NEED

mushrooms

paper

paints and brush

glue

coloured card

1 Cut one mushroom in half. Leave the rest whole but cut off the stems.

2 Paint the cut surfaces of the mushrooms.

3 Press them down onto your paper to make a print.

4 Create different patterns and mount your finished pictures on coloured card.

Woody skin

A fly trapped in amber, 40 million years old

THIN OR THICK-SKINNED?

Bark is made up of inner and outer layers. The inner layer is called the cambium. This is made up of millions of tiny building blocks called cells that are continually dividing. When these cells die they become the bark. Every year a new layer of bark is produced and the older layer is pushed to the outside. The bark of a tree can be as thin as 1 centimetre or as thick as 30 centimetres.

TREE-WATCHING

All plants need the gases oxygen and carbon dioxide. They breathe in and out through their trunks as well as their leaves. Examine the bark of a tree to see if you can spot the breathing holes called lenticles.

MADE BY BARK

The spice cinnamon is made from the bark of a tree that grows in India and Sri Lanka. Cinnamon is made by cutting the bark off young trees and then leaving it to dry. Cork is the bark of the cork oak. Every ten years or so, the outer layer is stripped away to leave the cambium. Cork is used to make things like bottle tops, shoes and furniture.

Did you know that trees have skin? It is called bark and is the outer layer of a tree or woody plant. And just like your skin, its job is to protect all the bits on the inside. As a tree grows, it gets too big for its outer skin. So the bark cracks, breaks and peels off, revealing a new layer of bark underneath.

CLUE TO THE PAST

Occasionally, nature allows us to glimpse the distant past by providing us with clues of its very own making. When tree trunks are damaged, a substance called resin oozes out to protect the wound. Insects, such as flies, sometimes become stuck in the resin. Fossilised resin is called amber and insects are sometimes preserved in the amber.

Bark rubbings

Plants

1 Place paper over the bark of a tree and rub gently with wax crayon.

2 Make rubbings of the grain of bark from different sorts of trees.

3 Mount your rubbings.

Tree markings produce 'groovy' patterns to brighten up your wall!

You can paint grainy tree-bark pictures too.

Fields of gold

If you were to fly above the vast, rolling plains of the USA, Russia, Canada and Australia on a warm summer's day, you would look down upon an endless carpet of gold. These countries grow most of the world's cereal crops, such as wheat, barley, maize, rice, oats and rye, in fields hundreds of times bigger than a football stadium.

BREAKFAST CEREAL

Cereals are grasses and we eat their seeds. Wheat is one of the most important cereal crops in the world. It is eaten every day, in some form or another, by more than a third of the world. We grow wheat to make bread, pasta, breakfast cereals and, of course, cakes and cookies.

FEEDING THE WORLD

Rice is the main food for half the world – more than 3 billion people. About 90 per cent of the world's rice is grown by hand in Asia. It is grown in paddy fields – special fields flooded with water.

AMAZING MAIZE

In steamy, hot, subtropical parts of the world, such as Central America, South America and Africa, maize, or sweet corn, is the main food. Maize can be ground into flour, or cornmeal, or eaten as a vegetable. It can have an amazing variety of colours, as well as speckles, spots and stripes.

HELPING THE LAND

The world's fertile farmland has to work very hard to feed the planet's ever growing population. Often the same crops are planted year after year on an enormous scale, over thousands of acres. When this happens the soil eventually loses its natural goodness. And because animals no longer graze on the land, providing the soil with essential nutrients in the form of dung, chemical fertilisers are often used instead. Many of today's farmers are trying to return to age-old farming methods, such as resting their fields for a year or two, allowing the soil to recover. And more and more farmers are growing crops without the aid of harmful chemicals, such as fertilisers.

Plants

black paint and brush

coloured felt

black pen

black felt-tip

rice or other small grain cereal

needle and thread

plastic bag

scissors

1 Fill a small plastic bag with rice and knot the end.

2 For the ladybird, cut 3 red felt ovals, each one slightly bigger than the bag of rice.

3 Sew 2 together with the bag inside.

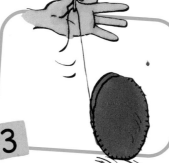

4 Cut 6 small strips and sew onto the bottom for the legs.

5 Use the third oval for the wings by cutting it in half and sewing the ends onto the top of the body.

6 Paint or draw eyes and black spots onto the felt.

Soft felt animals make perfect presents!

Make a mouse using two ovals of felt. Sew on ears, whiskers and a tail.

Sprouting seeds

It seems amazing that a tree can grow from a tiny seed. But even though most seeds are small, there's a lot packed inside. There's a baby plant and a supply of food to help it grow, and the seed is wrapped in a tough outer coat. Most seeds are produced by flowers and are contained in soft fruits such as tomatoes, oranges or apples.

LEAVING HOME

Plant seeds of different shapes, sizes and colours are transported away from their parent plant by the wind, rain and by a variety of animals. If they reach a spot where there is enough space, sunlight, water and nutrients, then they will start to grow, or germinate. In places where there are warm summers and cold winters, plant seeds that are released at the end of the summer often wait until spring to grow. This way they avoid the cold, sunless winter months.

GROWING UP

When a seed has found a suitable place to grow, a root breaks out of the seed coat and starts to take in water and minerals. Then a shoot pushes up through the soil towards the air and sunlight. Tiny leaves start to grow. They begin to make their own food using carbon dioxide, water and sunlight. The seed's job is done. The young plant now makes its own food. Some seedlings are so strong they can even push their way up through hard surfaces, such as tarmac, towards the sunlight.

RECORD HOLDERS

The length of time seeds can live without germinating varies. Willow seeds survive for just a few days. Some weeds can live for almost 50 years. But the champion seed is definitely the Arctic Lupin! Ten-thousand-year-old lupin seeds have germinated when given sunlight and water.

A seedling starts to grow.

Plants

Maraccas

1 Blow up two balloons.

2 Tear strips of newspaper, paste and cover the balloons. Leave to dry.

3 Cut the cardboard tubes, roll up tightly and tape.

Paste lengths of newspaper around the tubes as shown. **5**

Make a hole in the top of the maraccas. Tip in some rice and push in the tubes. **4**

6 When dry, paint the maraccas.

Now get together with friends and make music!

Shakers

Tear pieces of newspaper and paste them over the sides of the two tin cans. Cut out two circles of card to fit over the open ends. Pour rice into the tin cans and then glue on the card circle tops. Paint your shakers in bright colours and decorate by glueing on sequins.

13

Dwarf trees

Over a thousand years ago, people in China and Japan began to show their love and respect for nature by creating tiny replicas of trees and other plants. Their aim was to create miniature groves, forests or other natural landscapes. They grew the miniature plants in trays, so the art became known as 'bonsai' meaning 'tray-planted'. By the nineteenth century, bonsai was popular in Japanese homes, and today the interest has spread to countries worldwide.

TINY REPLICAS

Most bonsai trees are between five and nine centimetres tall. They are grown to look as much like a full-size tree as possible. Usually, bonsais with small leaves are grown. These include evergreens, such as cedar, pine and juniper, as well as fruit and flowering trees, such as plum, cherry and maple. Bonsai trees can be created from young trees, grown from seedlings, or kept small in their natural habitat and then planted in containers.

TIME AND PATIENCE

Bonsai growers need patience and time, as well as skill. The trees are kept small by constantly trimming the roots and branches and repotting them. The size of the container can affect the size of the tree. Shape and size are also controlled by pinching off new growth, bending the trunk and branches and training them with wire. The trees stay healthy by careful watering and fertilising. Bonsai trees can live for hundreds of years.

Plants

Miniature garden

Create a fabulous portable garden without even going outdoors!

WHAT YOU NEED

- small plastic sheet
- cardboard box
- paints
- sand
- pebbles
- small plants
- soil
- paintbrush
- shallow plastic lid

1 Paint your box in bright colours. Line it with a plastic sheet.

2 Fill the box with soil. Then make a path through it with the sand.

3 Use a plastic lid for a pond. Place pebbles around the outside of your garden and along the sides of the sandy path.

4 Plant a variety of small plants in the soil. Fill your pond with water.

Make sure you water your garden regularly. Plants need damp soil to grow.

Tropical beauties

Wonderfully scented, richly coloured orchids are among the most beautiful and unusual flowers in the world. Some are shaped like bees, some grow high up in trees and some feed on a fungus.

GROWING TOGETHER

Orchids are really rather clever. As well as growing in soil, they also grow on other plants. Wind-pollinating varieties of orchid grow on tree trunks. The wind carries the dust-like seeds through the steamy, tropical forest air. Many of the seeds fall onto tree trunks where they become attached to the bark. Some orchids cannot make their own food so, instead, they live on dead organic matter or are fed by a fungus living in their roots.

POLLINATION TRICKS

Some orchids have developed clever tricks to make sure that insects and birds carry pollen from one flower to another. Some have the most incredible scent, attracting all kinds of eager creatures. Others, such as the bee orchid, look remarkably like female bees. As a result, male bees try to mate with them and in doing so, carry the pollen between flowers.

VANILLA FLAVOUR

The flavouring vanilla is obtained from the seed pod of several species of orchid.

There are thousands of kinds of orchid growing in most parts of the world. They are found in large numbers in tropical rain forests.

Concertina orchids

WHAT YOU NEED

coloured paper

white paper

glue

tissue paper

scissors

newspaper

pencil

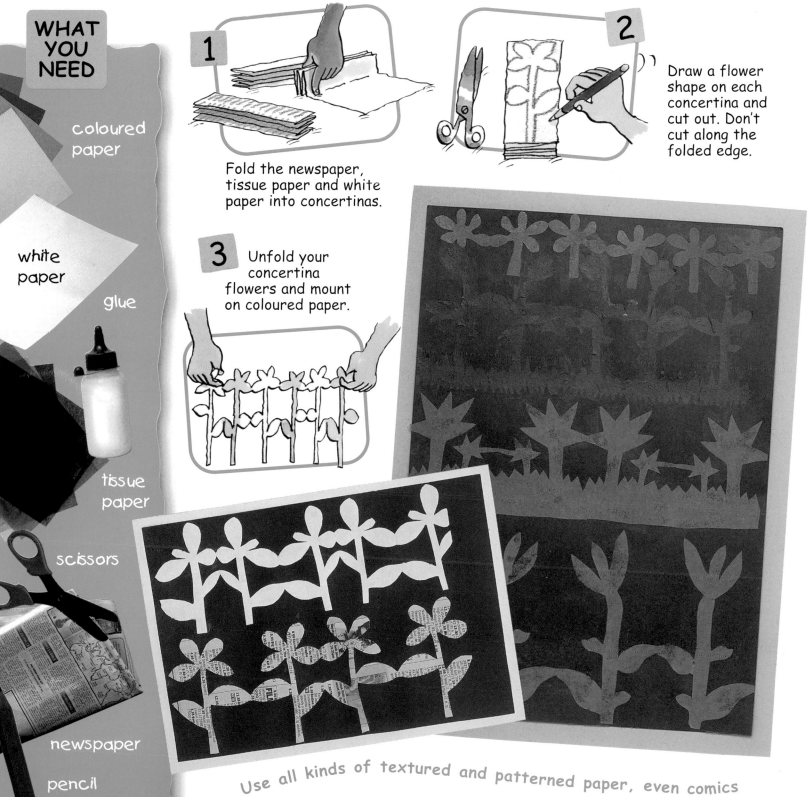

1 Fold the newspaper, tissue paper and white paper into concertinas.

2 Draw a flower shape on each concertina and cut out. Don't cut along the folded edge.

3 Unfold your concertina flowers and mount on coloured paper.

Use all kinds of textured and patterned paper, even comics

Gum and sap

Look around your home, especially your kitchen, your garden and your garage. There are probably lots of items made from a material called rubber. The tyres on your bicycle, some of the balls you play with, rubber gloves and elastic bands are all made from rubber.

COLLECTING RUBBER

Most of the world's natural rubber comes from rubber trees grown in Asia in special areas called plantations. Rubber is the gummy sap of the rubber tree. It is collected by tapping – making a cut in the bark and inserting a small tube. A white, milky liquid known as latex, that circulates through small veins in the inner bark, oozes out into a cup. Since the early 20th century, the main source of natural rubber has been the Brazilian rubber tree. This is a tall softwood tree with high, wide branches and a large area of bark. It is planted in rows on rubber plantations that cover enormous areas of land in Indonesia, Malaysia, Thailand, India, Vietnam, Sri Lanka and Nigeria.

MAKING RUBBER

After the latex is collected, it is processed for manufacturing. To soften it, it is passed between large rollers or rotating blades. It is then mixed with other chemicals to strengthen and stiffen it. Latex is also treated to withstand heat and cold. Then it is pressed into large sheets. The sheets are cut and shaped and exported as rubber to manufacturers around the world.

Rubber is collected from a rubber tree by tapping.

Rubber band harp

WHAT YOU NEED

- newspaper
- paint and brush
- cardboard
- sequins
- glitter
- big cardboard tube
- rubber bands
- glue
- scissors

1 Cut the cardboard tube, as shown, leaving the circular base intact.

2 Glue lengths of rubber bands from one end to the other.

3 Make the frame from cardboard pieces, as shown. Glue around the tube.

4 Paste on strips of newspaper. When dry, paint.

5 Decorate with sequins and glitter.

Twang the strings and have fun making music!

19

Opening petals

Have you ever wondered why there are so many different colours, shapes and types of flowers? And why they smell so nice? Flowers have vibrant colours and beautiful smells in order to attract insects, birds and other small animals. These winged visitors ensure that pollen is transferred from one plant to another.

All about pollination

A plant's main job is to produce seeds that grow into new plants. For this to happen, a fine powder called pollen from the male part of a flower, the stamen, must be transferred to the female part of another flower, the stigma. This process is called pollination. Animals, especially insects, and the wind and rain all help to transfer pollen.

Visit me!

Flowering plants have different ways of encouraging pollination. Some have brightly coloured petals and wonderful scents. But most attract insects with a sweet liquid food called nectar. As insects drink the nectar, they brush against the pollen, which sticks to their bodies and then falls off on to the next flower. The pollen fertilises the flower's seeds so they can grow into new plants.

Favourite colours and perfumes

Bees tend to visit yellow, blue and blue-green flowers that open during the day. Butterflies are attracted to beautifully scented flowers. They especially like buddleia, milkweed and verbena.

Yellow pollen can be seen on the tips of the stamen of these flowers.

Plants

Sunflower

1 Cut out a circle of card to make the centre of your sunflower. Cut out two much larger circles from two sheets of yellow tissue paper.

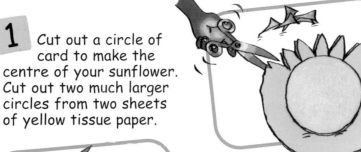

2 Place the card circle in the centre of a tissue paper circle. Cut petal shapes around the edge. Repeat with the second circle.

3 Glue one yellow flower on either side of the card circle, so that the petal shapes frame the edge and overlap each other.

4 Scrunch up brown and orange tissue paper and silver foil into little balls. Glue these onto the card circle to form the centre of your sunflower.

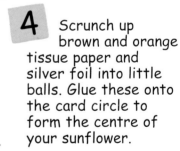

Make lots of sunflowers, and tape a stick to the back of each, then put them in a big vase

21

Plant juice

Have you ever wondered how your sweater became red or your trousers blue? Well, clothes are stained using special substances called dyes. Until about 150 years ago all dyes came from plants and animals. Today, chemicals are used.

CHANGING COLOUR

Most of the dyes we have today are made from chemicals in large factories around the world. There are now over 3,000 different dye colours. But for more than 5,000 years, less than 100 natural dye colours were available.

MAGICAL BLUE

For over 2,000 years in many parts of the world, blue dye was taken from the woad plant. Woad was also a healing plant and when ancient warriors dyed their clothes and their skin with blue dye before a battle, it not only terrified the enemy but it helped to heal their wounds as well.

REDDER THAN RED

Red dye was made from the madder root or from dried insects that live on the kermes oak. As Turkey was one of the main countries to use the madder root to make the dye, the vibrant colour became known as Turkey red.

Tie dye t-shirt

Plants

rubber bands

tea bags

T-shirt

inks

bowl or pan

water

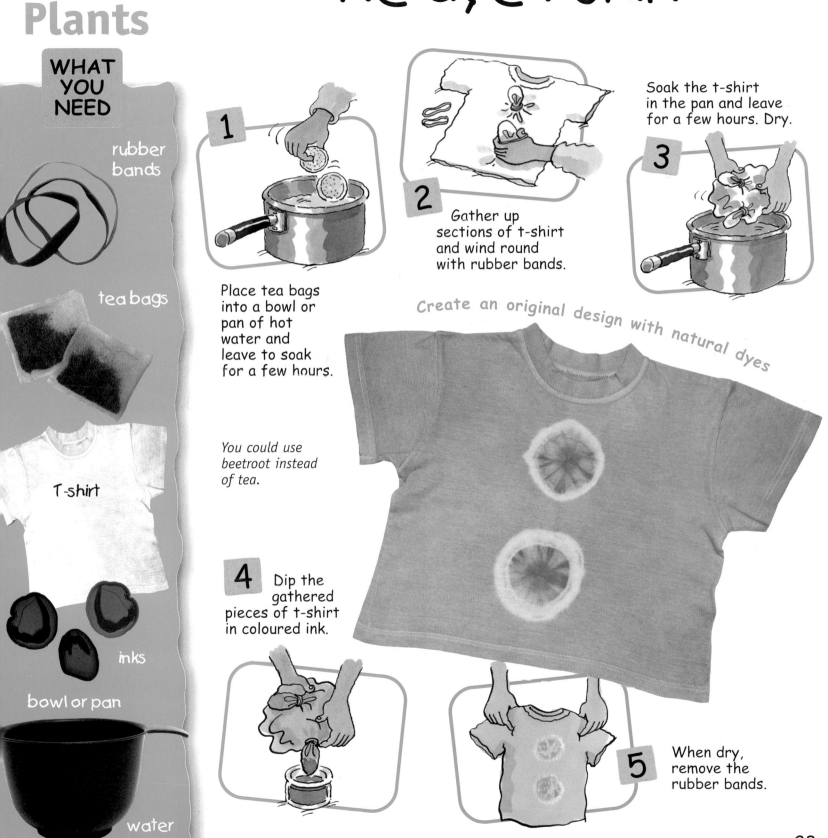

1 Place tea bags into a bowl or pan of hot water and leave to soak for a few hours.

2 Gather up sections of t-shirt and wind round with rubber bands.

Soak the t-shirt in the pan and leave for a few hours. Dry.

3

Create an original design with natural dyes

You could use beetroot instead of tea.

4 Dip the gathered pieces of t-shirt in coloured ink.

5 When dry, remove the rubber bands.

Circles of time

As you grow, your arms and legs become longer and your body length increases. Each year you become a little taller and wider. Trees grow in much the same way. Their branches grow outwards and then become rounder. Their trunks widen a little with each passing year. And like you, food, water and sunlight keep them healthy and help them to grow.

HOW OLD ARE YOU?

Trees can live for hundreds of years. Some, such as America's Californian redwoods, are thousands of years old. You can tell how old a tree is by counting the tree rings inside the trunk. Each ring represents one year's growth.

SLOW, QUICK, QUICK, SLOW!

Some trees have rings that are very close together. This means that weather and soil conditions were not good enough for these trees to grow very much. But when the growth rings are farther apart, the trees have been able to grow quite quickly.

PETRIFIED WOOD

Wood will eventually die and decay. But if it dies in peat or a bog, it can become petrified wood. This means that bogs or peat preserve the shape of the wood even though it is dead. Petrified forests can look a little scary. Dead trunks and branches with eerie shapes, frozen in time, rise up from a bog making it look like an alien landscape.

Petrified wood is wood that has turned into rock.

Plants

WHAT YOU NEED

card

scissors

glitter

pencil

sequins

wood shavings

gold paint and brush

cocktail sticks

glue

gold thread and needle

Spiral mobile

1 Draw a circle on a piece of card. Starting from the middle, draw a spiral shape inside the circle. Cut out along the lines.

2 Paint one side and decorate with sequins.

3 Stick assorted woodshavings on the other side and decorate with cocktail sticks, glitter, sequins and paint. Leave to dry.

4 Make a hole in the middle of the spiral circle and attach a length of golden thread.

5 Hang from the ceiling.

Hang the spiral in an open window and watch it slowly turn round in the breeze

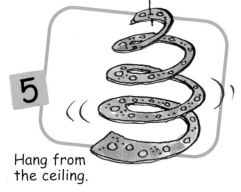

25

Fancy fossils

DINOSAUR FOOD

Whenever you go to an evergreen forest, you are visiting the Earth as it was millions of years ago. Evergreens are the descendants of ancient trees that were once fed on by early plant-eating dinosaurs. The prehistoric forests included redwood, yew, pine, cypress and monkey puzzle trees.

PRIMITIVE PLANTS

Horsetails and ferns were also an important food for plant-eating dinosaurs. They grew quickly, and formed enormous, swampy forests. It wasn't until the end of the Jurassic period, 140 million years ago, that flowering plants first appeared. Then, because they could spread their seeds more easily, they began to take over as the Earth's dominant plants.

STRANGE OR FAMILIAR?

If we could go back in time millions of years, we would see some strange plants but many that we might recognise as well. Cycads were early seed plants that looked like palm trees with woody trunks and tough leaves. Ginkgoes were tall fern-like trees that grew in high places. You can still see descendants of these plants today – slender, ornamental ginkgoes with fan-shaped leaves are often grown along city streets.

Millions of years ago when the first dinosaurs lived, the Earth was a very different place. Colourful flowering plants were nowhere to be seen, and huge forests covered much of the green landscape. Some ancient plants still exist today, while others have disappeared for ever. Our only images of them are imprinted in their fossils.

FROZEN IN TIME

Fossils tell us what ancient plants looked like. A fossil forms when a plant or animal dies. If it falls into mud or sand, it may be preserved when the mud or sand turns into rock over millions of years.

Leaf tiles

Plants

WHAT YOU NEED

clay

paints and brush

silver and gold paint

leaves

1 Soften your clay, then make several flat, square shapes.

2 Place a leaf on one tile and rub evenly across it. Peel off the leaf to reveal the print. Leave to dry.

3 On another tile, use the wooden end of your paintbrush to make a leaf pattern. Leave to dry.

4 Paint your tiles.

Make lots of different leaf patterns

27

Tree nurseries

We could not survive without trees. They 'breathe in' harmful carbon dioxide and 'breathe out' the oxygen humans and animals need to stay alive. And forests give food and shelter to thousands of people, birds, animals, insects and plants. In the past, we destroyed trees and forests without thinking. Now we are careful to grow new trees to replace the ones that are lost.

REPLANTING RAINFORESTS

For many years, vast areas of rainforest were cut down for wood, or burnt to make space for farming. But the destroyed forests were gone forever. Today, countries have started to look after their forests. Tree nurseries have been set up, so that new trees are always growing. When they are big enough, the young trees are planted in the cleared, or empty forest areas. In this way, the plants and animals that live in forest habitats are protected.

TREE HOUSES

Animals and plants need their leafy habitats to survive. Many animals such as monkeys, birds and bats find food and shelter high up in the trees. Other creatures such as insects, rodents, rabbits and snakes make their homes underground among tree roots. Many animals feed on the plants that grow among the trees. Plants need good soil to grow in. It is made richer by the leaves that fall from the trees. Their roots also hold the soil in place. Without trees, many forest plants die out.

NEW LIFE

A forest that has been destroyed by fire can quickly recover. In hot, dry weather a forest fire may burn for days, destroying thousands of kilometres of woodland. But in a few months, new seedlings begin to sprout up from the burned and blackened ground. Slowly, the trees begin to grow and the animals, birds, insects and plants can return to a new forest home.

Woodland warren

Build an underground scene of rabbits at home

Plants

WHAT YOU NEED

large cardboard box

scissors

newspaper

paints and brush

card

small pebbles

corrugated card

cardboard tube

glue

pencil

clay

coloured paper

1 Cut out one side of the box. Cut a hole in the top of the box. Slot the small cardboard tube into it.

2 Scrunch newspaper into balls and glue inside the box.

3 Glue half tubes of corrugated card in among the newspaper for tunnels. Leave 2 or 3 empty spaces.

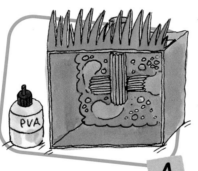

4 When dry, paint and glue on pebbles. Cut out a strip of grass from card. Paint and glue it onto the box.

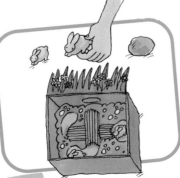

5 Shape rabbits from clay. When dry, paint them and place in your mini warren.

Stick cut-out paper flowers and leaves amongst the grass.

29

Hardy plants

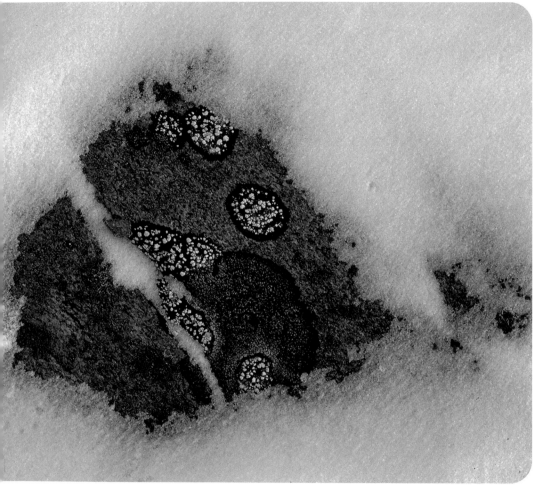

The lichen here, which is growing on rock, can survive even in ice and snow.

In the vast, dry, sandy deserts of the world the climate is very hot. While on the Arctic tundra, the weather is so cold that the land is covered with snow and ice for most of the year. Most plants cannot survive in these extreme conditions, but there are some that have learned to live in the toughest places.

ON THE TUNDRA

For two or three months during the warmer summer months, the frozen tundra thaws a little. Surface ice melts, although the ground below remains frozen solid. Tundra flowering plants, such as stitchwort, cranberries and dwarf birch, spring up from the soil. And colourful lichens, mosses, herbs and grasses burst into life. Most tundra plants are small and grow close to the ground to protect themselves from bitter, icy winds.

CLEVER LICHENS

Lichens are amazing because they can live in the harshest conditions. They are the only plants growing near the extreme North and South poles. During the cold Arctic months, they provide reindeer with food.

WATER GATHERERS

In the desert it rains very rarely, and in sudden large downpours. That is why succulent plants, such as cacti and spurge, have shallow roots that spread out a long way to quickly soak up as much water as possible. They also have large fleshy stems for storing water over long periods of time.

PRICKLY PLANTS

A long time ago cacti had leaves instead of prickles. But leaves release too much moisture into the air. So slowly, over millions of years, cacti developed prickles, or spines, to help keep moisture in.

Plants

Cactus desk tidy

WHAT YOU NEED

1 large and 2 small cardboard tubes

newspaper

scissors

paint and brush

glue

tape

cocktail sticks

glitter

box lid

1 Use the box lid as your base and tape the large cardboard tube in one corner.

2 Glue scrunched up newspaper onto the base to make different sized containers.

3 Cut two holes in the sides of the big cardboard tube and insert two smaller ones.

4 Glue bits of scrunched newspaper for knobbly bits onto your cactus. Then glue strips of newspaper all over it and leave to dry.

5 Paint and decorate with glitter. Push cocktail sticks into the cactus to give it a spiky look.

Store pens, pencils and paintbrushes safely in this prickly pot!

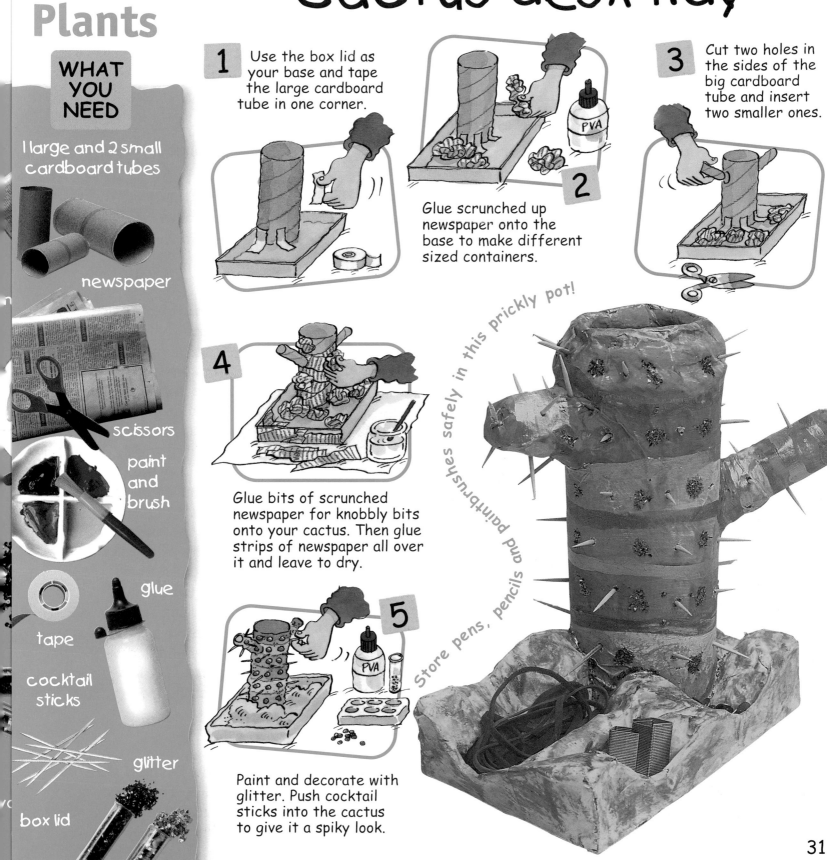

31

Paper and pulp

Did you know that your favourite comic book, storybook or magazine began life as a tree in a large forest a long way from where you live? How does a tall, leafy tree become the pages of a book? Let's find out.

THE JOURNEY BEGINS

The main ingredient used in paper-making is wood. Trees are cut down and transported to sawmills. There the wood is cut up to make lots of products. Wood chips are usually all that's left of the tree. These wood chips are used to make paper.

TURN TO PULP

Enormous trucks piled high with wood chips carry their load to paper mills. After the chips have been cleaned, they travel along a series of pipes and tubes to be made into pulp in large machines called refiners. Using water, steam and large spinning discs, the wood chips become pulp.

ON THE WIRE

The pulp, which is mostly water, is then put on to a fast-moving screen called a wire. Here the water is taken out of the pulp by pumps and the pulp is pressed into sheets of paper. Then it is dried. Next, the paper is ironed or smoothed for printing and then wound on to a giant roll. The paper is later cut to the size requested by customers.

DELIVERY TIME

Once the paper is cut, trucks or trains transport it to destinations all over the world. Then the paper becomes your favourite book or comic.

Handmade paper

Plants

WHAT YOU NEED

absorbent dishcloth

water and bowl

paint

straw

glitter

newspaper   wire mesh

grass   leaves

1 Tear up some newspaper and place in a large bowl of water. Leave it to soak overnight.

2 Drain and transfer the newspaper pulp to another bowl. Add paint for colour.

3 Slide the wire mesh into the pulp and lift it out. Place on top of newspaper.

4 Press down hard all over with a dishcloth to flatten the pulp.

Flip the pulp over. Remove the mesh and leave to dry.

5

You can make a collage from your homemade paper

Adding glitter, leaves or other items to the pulp will give your paper an interesting texture.

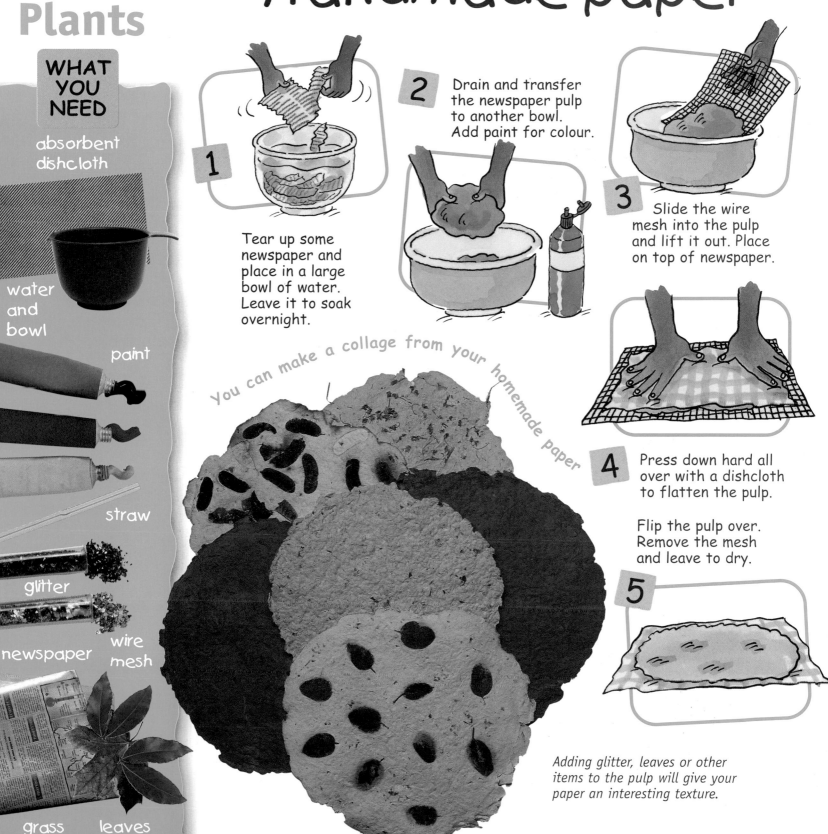

Dropping leaves

Have you ever wondered why leaves change colour? Some trees that grow where the winter is cold lose their leaves in order to survive the freezing weather. Before dropping from the trees, the leaves turn yellow or orange because water stops reaching them. The leaves slowly die, turning brown before falling to the ground.

AUTUMN LEAVES

Trees that shed their leaves in winter are known as deciduous trees. They grow in parts of the world where the climate is temperate, such as southern parts of Europe, North America and Asia.

Oak, maple, ash, birch and beech are all deciduous trees that sleep during the chilly winter months. In the heart of winter, their branches are bare. Then, in the early spring, these trees burst into life and new buds and blossoms appear. As the weather warms up, leaves and fruits start to grow.

EVERGREENS

Some trees do not change colour in the autumn, or drop their leaves during the winter. These trees are known as evergreens and include fir, spruce, pine and cypress. They are very tough plants that hold on to the water stored inside them. So when winter comes and water in the ground turns to ice, they still have a store of water to live on.

NO SEASONS

In the tropical rainforests that grow on or near the equator, conditions are sunny, warm and wet and trees can grow all year round. Most trees are evergreens, but there are deciduous trees as well. Deciduous trees that grow here do not drop their leaves all at once. They replace them, one by one, as they drop off.

Deciduous trees are bare during the freezing winter months.

Four seasons collage

Give each tree a seasonal look

WHAT YOU NEED

scissors

wire

paint and brush

card

mounting card

tissue paper

glue

textured papers

sequins

pencil

cotton wool

glitter

1 Draw an outline of a tree trunk with branches on the card and cut out.

2 Using the cutout tree as a template, draw four trees on separate pieces of paper.

3 Cut out pieces of textured paper and glue onto the trunks.

4 Paint the backgrounds. Cut leaf shapes from the seasonally-coloured tissue paper and glue onto your trees.

Spring

Summer

Autumn

Winter

Cotton wool blossoms

Wind wire around a twig. Glue pieces of cotton wool and green tissue onto the wire and woody branches. Now decorate your cotton wool blossoms with glitter.

Exploding spores

If you stroll through a shady woodland or a dark forest – in fact anywhere where it is damp – you will find mosses, ferns, lichens and liverworts. They are all ancient plant varieties: in fact, many of them were around millions of years ago at the time of the dinosaurs. They are known as non-flowering plants because they have no flowers and make spores instead of seeds.

VELVETY MOSS

In damp, sunless places you can see carpets of green velvet moss growing. If you were to take a good look at a piece of moss, you would see lots of slender stems covered with minute green leaves. Underneath are tiny hairs that attach themselves to the ground. On the stalks above the leaves are teardrop-shaped capsules containing tiny spores. The capsules burst and the spores are carried away by the wind. New mosses grow where they land.

FEATHERY FERNS

Thousands of years ago, plant-eating dinosaurs munched on ferns. Many ferns have feather-like leaves, or fronds, that are divided into lots of little leaflets. Ferns form spores on the underside of their leaves. The stems of most ferns grow underground.

LIVERWORTS AND LICHENS

Liverworts produce spores that develop inside little capsules. Lichens are really two plants living together – a fungus and an alga. The alga supplies the fungus with food. The fungus protects the alga and gives it water.

A moss capsule explodes, releasing a cloud of spores.

Fern forest

WHAT YOU NEED

a collection of ferns

paints and brush

white card and paper

black card

gold paint

white paint

2 Collect a handful of ferns. Paint one side of some ferns with dark greens and blues and some ferns in violet and black.

1 Paint a pale green and yellow background onto white card.

3 Put the green and blue-painted ferns face down on the background. Place another piece of paper over the top of them and gently rub over the leaves.

4 Remove the paper to reveal the prints. Now lay the violet and black-painted ferns over the top and repeat the printing exercise for a shadowy forest effect.

Use ferns to print decorative borders on your personal mail

You can make a snowy scene by printing white and gold ferns onto black card.

Medicine plants

A field of purple lavender

What would you think if your doctor gave you peppermint for your headache or ginger if you felt sick? Long ago, that is what would have happened – you would have been given plants to make you feel better. Many of these plants are still used as medicines today.

THEN AND NOW

The plants used as ancient medicine, such as lavender or ginseng, were grown in special gardens, and people known as herbalists wrote about what the medicines could do in books called herbals. Today, science and nature work together. Many modern medicines contain plant ingredients as well as ingredients made by people. Scientists journey through the forests of the world, examining thousands of plants in search of new cures.

ESSENTIAL OILS

Ancient herbalists used plant oils to heal wounds and infections. The oils, just like today, were taken from the flowers, fruits, bark and roots of plants and trees. Oils taken from the plants aloe vera and jojoba are still used for skin problems.

HEALING POWER

Native North Americans used the bark and leaves of the witch hazel plant to heal injuries such as cuts and swelling. They also used parts of the white willow to cure a variety of aches and pains. So it's hardly surprising that modern scientists used the leaves and bark of the white willow to make the very first form of aspirin.

Fragrant forest

Plants

WHAT YOU NEED

herbs and spices

paintbrush

twigs

black or grey card

glue

gold paint

1 Glue twigs onto the card to make tree trunks and branches.

2 Use all kinds of spices to create different sorts of foliage on the trees. Glue them in place.

3 When dry, add gold paint to the background for a highlighting effect.

Create a scented woodland scene that shimmers and shines

Glossary and Index

alga (plural: algae) A simple sea plant, such as seaweed. 38

amber The resin squeezed from a tree that might be millions of years old. 8

bark The tough outer layer of a tree or woody plant. 8, 16, 18, 42

barley 10

blossom 36

bog 24

bonsai A miniature tree specially developed in Japan. 14

branch 14, 24, 36

cactus (plural: cacti) A spiny, prickly plant that needs very little water to grow. 30

cambium The inner layer of bark from which new wood and bark grow. 8

carbon dioxide The gas taken in by plants. 4, 8, 12, 28

cell The smallest part of a living thing. Cells can grow, feed and reproduce. 4, 8

cereal A grass, the seeds of which are used for food. Wheat, rice, barley, maize and oats are all cereals. 10, 30, 32

chemical 10, 18, 22

chlorophyll Green pigment, or colouring, that plants use to make food from sunlight. 4, 6

chloroplast The tiny part of a green plant that contains chlorophyll. 4

cork 8

crop Cereals and other foods grown by farmers. 10

cultivate To grow plants for food. 32

deciduous Plants that drop their leaves during cold winters. 4, 36

dye The juices from plants can be used to make dyes. Woad is a blue dye, madder root is a red dye. 22

evergreen Plants that have leaves all year round. 4, 14, 26, 36

farming The cultivation of land to produce foodstuffs. 10

fern 38

fertilise To combine the male cell with the female cell to form a seed. 10, 14, 20

flower The part of a plant that has brightly coloured petals. 12, 16, 20, 26, 32, 38, 42

forest 14, 16, 26, 28, 34, 42

fossil The remains of a living thing, preserved in rock. 8, 26

fruit The part of a flowering plant that contains the seeds. Apples, aubergines, tomatoes, oranges and pears are all fruits. 6, 12, 14, 32, 36, 40, 42

fungus (plural: fungi) A simple plant that does not contain chlorophyll. Mushrooms and toadstools are fungi. 6, 16, 32

germinate To grow from a seed or spore. 12

gourd Pumpkins, melons and cucumbers are gourds. 32

grass 10, 30, 32

habitat The surroundings in which a plant lives. 28

herb An aromatic plant used in cookery and medicine. Peppermint and dandelion are herbs. 30, 40, 42

latex The white, milky liquid of the rubber tree which is tapped to make rubber. 18

leaf 4, 8, 30, 32, 36, 38, 44

lenticle The breathing holes in the surface of tree bark. 8

lichen 30, 38

liverwort 38

maize 10

medicine A substance used to treat illness. Some plants, such as lavender and ginseng, are used to make medicine. 42

mineral One of many chemicals, such as iron, needed by plants. 12

moss 30, 38

mushroom 6

nectar A sweet liquid made by flowers to attract insects to them. 20, 44

nut 32

nutrient Nutrients are the good things found in food that help animals and plants live and grow. 10, 12, 44

oil Oils taken from plants can be used in medicine and cookery. Aloe vera and jojoba provide healing oils. 42

orchid 16

organic Something that comes from living things. 16

oxygen The essential gas given off by all plants. 8, 28

paddy field A water-flooded field cut into a hillside, especially in Asia where rice is grown. 10

peat A swampy area where very old trees were pressed down into water and minerals as they died. 24

petal 20

petrified forest Ancient trees that have been preserved in a bog or peat and have turned to stone. 24

photosynthesis The process by which plants use sunlight to turn water and carbon dioxide into food. 4

pigment A word for a colouring. 6

plantation An area where trees or crops have been planted for harvesting. 18

pod The part of a plant that encloses the seeds. 16

poisonous plant 6

pollen A yellow powder made by a plant's stamens, containing the male cells. 16, 20

pollination The transfer of pollen from the male part of one flower to the female part of another. 16

pulp Watery ground-up wood. 34

rainforest A thick evergreen forest with heavy rainfall all year. 28, 36

resin A substance which oozes out of the bark of a tree to protect a wound. 8

rice 10, 32

rings The circular marks within the trunk of a tree that mark the years it has taken to grow. 24

root 4, 14, 28, 32, 42

rubber 18

sap The juice that flows through a tree, carrying water and food. 18

scent 16, 20

seaweed 32

seed The part of a flowering plant that will grow into a new plant. Nuts and beans are seeds. 6, 10, 12, 14, 16, 20, 28, 32, 38, 40

soil The top layer of earth, in which plants grow. 10, 12, 16, 24, 28, 44

spice Aromatic plant used in medicine and cookery. 8, 16, 42

spore A tiny cell produced by ferns, mosses and fungi that grows into a new plant. 6, 38

stamen The male part of a flower. 20

starch The food created and stored in the parts of a plant. 4

stem 4, 32, 38

stigma The tip of the female part of a flower. 20

stomata Tiny holes on the underside of a leaf. 4

sugar 4

sunlight 4, 6, 12, 24

temperate A mild climate, between the hot tropics and cold poles. 36

toadstool 6

tree Cedar, birch, cherry, fir, pine, cypress, palm, ginkgo, spruce, oak and willow are all trees. 8, 14, 16, 18, 24, 28, 34

trunk 8, 14, 16, 24

tundra A large snow-covered area of land on the edge of the Arctic, where no trees grow. 30

vegetable A plant or part of a plant that can be eaten. Aubergines, cassava, beans, broccoli and squashes are all vegetables. 32, 40

vine 44

water 4, 12, 14, 20, 24, 36, 38, 44

weed 12

wheat 10, 32